TALES FROM THE PITCH

LIONEL MESSI

HARRY CONINX

RAVEN

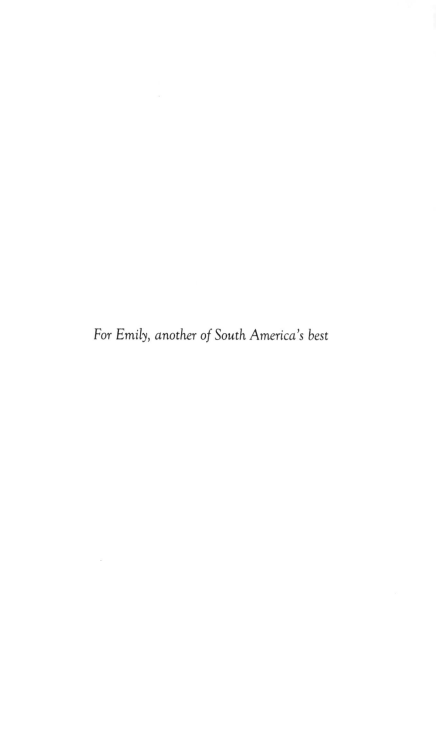

For Emily, another of South America's best

CONTENTS

I

CARNIVAL IN RIO

July 2021, Maracanã Stadium, Rio de Janeiro, Brazil
Copa América Final, Argentina v Brazil

"Remember the last time we were here?" Lionel asked, turning towards Ángel Di María as they stood in the tunnel. "It was so different then."

"I was injured!" Di María replied. "I didn't play."

"Oh yeah," Lionel replied quietly. "We needed you then."

His mind drifted back to that game seven years ago.

It wasn't actually the last time he'd played at the Estádio do Maracanã, but he hadn't needed to explain that to Ángel. He'd known exactly which game he'd meant.

The 2014 World Cup Final.

It had been the closest Argentina had gone to winning the trophy in over 20 years, since the days of Diego Maradona. It had been a very different atmosphere that day, not least because there were so many more fans in the stadium.

So many Argentinian fans had made the trip over to Brazil to get behind the team that day, that it had practically felt like a home game.

Lionel remembered the chances that had fallen at his feet, and the one he'd put wide. He remembered Gonzalo Higuaín dragging an effort wide.

And he couldn't help but see Mario Götze volleying into the back of the net, and the celebrations of the German players and fans. Even as he'd collected his award for Player of the Tournament, he'd been in tears. It had been the lowest moment of his career.

And now he was back in the same stadium – the stadium that had marked that low point.

Could he now make it a stadium to mark one of his highest points?

"I wasn't sure we'd ever be back here," Di María said.

He was one of the few players remaining from the squad that had finished runners-up in 2014. Just him, Lionel and Sergio Agüero.

"I didn't think we'd ever get another chance," Di María added.

Lionel nodded. The 2014 final wasn't the only serious disappointment they'd experienced. They'd lost the final of this competition in 2015 and 2016, and Lionel had had an additional defeat in 2007. Four finals with his country – and four defeats.

Both of them had won so much at club level, but the one thing missing from their trophy collection was an international trophy. Now, today, they had one more chance.

But they were up against the team that had denied them so many times, and they were in the stadium that had witnessed their lowest ebb. Could they pull it off?

"How are you doing, Leo?"

It was Brazil's star striker and Lionel's former

Barcelona team-mate Neymar. He leaned over and slapped Lionel on the back.

"Good luck today," he said, smiling.

Neymar had the easy confidence of someone who'd already won an international trophy with his country. He didn't have the pressure that Lionel felt on his own shoulders.

"Good luck," Lionel replied.

His voice sounded small, especially in the mainly empty and cavernous Maracanã stadium. The COVID-19 pandemic meant that only a small number of fans had been allowed in, and the noise was nothing compared to seven years ago.

For the first 20 minutes, the game was cagey, tight, with neither side dominating. Brazil and Argentina were historic rivals and neither side wanted to lose this game. Neither side wanted to give the other anything to cheer about.

At first, Lionel was little more than a bystander, watching on. But then it changed. A long ball from Rodrigo De Paul drifted in behind the Brazil defence to where Ángel Di María had burst through.

He controlled the bouncing ball with an exquisite first touch and then dinked it over the onrushing Ederson. The ball bounced into the back of the net.

Goal! Argentina were ahead!

"Great finish, Ángel!" Lionel shouted, grabbing his friend. "I knew we could have done with you in 2014!"

"I'm learning from the best," Di María replied, a huge smile on his face.

As the goal celebrations continued, Lionel turned to calm the players down.

"There's over an hour left, lads," he said. "We've got one goal. We need another, because we know they're going to come back at us. We're going to have to work hard. This game isn't done yet."

The players nodded. He was the captain and it was his job to keep them all focused. They also knew just how much a win today would mean to him.

Argentina controlled most of the first half, with Lautaro Martínez going close. Going into half-time, they felt relatively comfortable. But they knew that Brazil had the players to change the game, players that could score goals.

Neymar began to pull the strings for Brazil in the second half and, once more, Lionel found himself almost a bystander, looking on as Richarlison and Gabriel Barbosa forced Argentinan keeper Martínez into making a number of key saves.

And then, with just a couple of minutes left, Lionel's moment came. The ball was fed into him and he was just a few yards away from goal. He took a touch, starting to plan his move, planning to dance his way round the keeper.

But his own feet betrayed him. The ball squirmed loose and Ederson flipped it away. Lionel sunk to the floor, desperately sticking out a leg to where the ball had been, but knowing it had gone.

Was that his last chance to score, gone? Had he let his country down?

The remaining minutes seemed to last for hours. The Argentina players were desperate for the ref to blow his whistle, to call time on the final.

Then, at last it came, the moment that had been in Lionel's dreams for 16 years, since he'd made his Argentina debut. He had won a trophy with his country.

Finally he could get his hands on a major competition, wearing the blue and white of Argentina.

This was the one thing that had been missing from his CV, the one thing that had stopped people from calling him the greatest player in the world. And now he had it.

For most players, this would be the pinnacle of their careers, the final moment of success. But Lionel was already looking forward. There was a World Cup next year, and he had a season coming up with his new club, PSG.

He wasn't done yet. This was his first international trophy, but it most certainly wasn't the last trophy of his career.

He was determined to do more.

2
MAKING UP THE NUMBERS

March 1993, Rosario, Argentina

"Are you going to watch your brothers today?" Lionel's grandmother asked him as she drove him to the match.

Lionel nodded. He would often play alongside his older brothers, Rodrigo and Matias, in the streets around their house, or in the local park.

Lionel was a lot smaller than his brothers, but playing

with them had only improved his skills. He needed plenty of tricks to keep the ball away from them.

"How come you're not playing today?" his grandma asked.

"I'm not big enough to play for Rosario yet."

"It's not all about size," his gran told him. "I've seen you boys play and – don't tell the others this – I think you're better."

"Really?" Lionel replied with a grin. He was always happy to hear how good he was at football, but he'd always thought that his brothers were better than him.

"Absolutely. Is it *just* that you think you're too small? Or is there something else?"

Lionel started to say something, but changed his mind. He didn't want to admit to his grandma how he really felt.

"You can tell me, Leo," she said, sensing his anxiety.

"I'm scared," he said quietly after a pause. "I'm worried I'll get injured, or that I won't make friends in the team. What if I mess up and people get angry?"

"It's OK to make mistakes, Leo. There's nobody in the world who hasn't messed up at some point in their lives. All footballers make mistakes. But it's about how you come back from them. It's how you deal with it."

Lionel just stared out of the window.

"Leo, I really believe that you can be the best player in the world, but you have to believe in yourself," his gran continued. "Maybe not today, but soon, you'll have to leave the streets and get on the football pitch. Just know that, whatever happens, your family will be completely behind you."

Lionel nodded. He was still nervous about playing. It wasn't about being on the pitch that scared him. When the ball was at his feet, he felt comfortable – relaxed and at ease. Everything just seemed natural to him.

It was when he didn't have the ball that he was more nervous. Talking to the players, the coaches, trying to make friends ... These were the things he found intimidating and that he was worried about.

"You're sure you don't want to join Rodrigo and Matias?" his gran asked, as they arrived at the park. He could see his brothers already out on the pitch.

Lionel shook his head and wandered over to where his parents were standing on the sidelines.

"It looks like we're a player down," his mum said.

"What?"

A quick glance around the pitch proved his mum was right. There were only six players in his brothers' team.

Just then, the team's coach, Salvador, marched over to Lionel's parents and exchanged a couple of words with his mum and dad. Then he pointed at Lionel.

"What's going on?" Lionel asked his grandma.

"They want you to make up the numbers," she grinned. "This is your chance, Leo!"

He gulped nervously as Salvador crouched down in front of him.

"You fancy it then, little man?" he asked. "You don't even need to *do* anything – just be out there so we have the numbers."

"He'll do more than that," his grandmother said, giving Lionel a sly wink.

Before Lionel was given a chance to reply, Salvador led him out onto the pitch, alongside his older brothers.

"Come on, Leo, show everyone what you can do," Matias shouted encouragingly.

Straight from kick-off, the ball rolled towards Lionel's

feet. He wanted to control it, but he froze and the ball carried on past him.

"You're better than that, mate!" Rodrigo called to him as he ran after it.

A few moments later, Matias passed to Lionel. Suddenly, he heard his grandmother's words repeating in his head. This was his big moment to prove himself.

Lionel controlled the ball and dribbled up the pitch, skipping past challenges as he went.

Salvador's jaw fell open as he watched Lionel moving up the pitch. The young player was almost knocked to the floor by a defender, but somehow he just kept on moving. It was as if the ball was glued to his feet.

As the goal came into sight, Lionel struck the ball hard and low. It skipped off the ground and rolled past the keeper into the net.

Lionel jumped into the air as his brothers and team-mates celebrated with him. Even the other team's players congratulated him, impressed by the goal.

As Lionel walked back towards the half-way line, he looked at his grandma and smiled, as she mouthed the words, *I love you!*

It was an unexpected beginning, but at the age of five, Lionel's football career had begun.

3

THE MACHINE OF '87

July 1999, Buenos Aires, Argentina

"They're all watching you," Franco said to Lionel with a grin. Lionel followed his friend's gaze and looked over to the large group of people gathered on the other side of the pitch.

"Not just for me," Lionel answered. "They're here for all of us: The Machine of '87."

After Lionel's magical first moments playing

alongside his brothers, he'd quickly been snapped up by Newell's Old Boys, the big local team. Since then, he'd scored almost 500 goals as part of what people called "The Machine of '87" – the unbeatable youth generation of Newell's Old Boys.

The team had since become famous in the local area and were often invited to the senior team's matches to entertain the crowd at half-time, with a show of tricks and skills.

In fact, The Machine of '87 were so good that many people believed they were watching the future Argentinian national team.

Another of Lionel and Franco's team-mates, Sergio, overheard their conversation.

"Don't be stupid, Leo," he laughed. "You're the next Maradona. They're here for *you*."

"Look, I'm only 12. I'm not going to be Maradona."

"If you're not going to be the next Maradona, well, you're going to be the first Lionel Messi," Franco replied with a smile.

"Remember us when you've made it to the top," Sergio grinned.

"I'll never forget you guys, you know that. But if there's one thing I'm never going to be, it's big!" Lionel said, as all three boys burst into laughter.

Lionel had always been small for his age. His quick feet, explosive acceleration and keen eye for a pass all made up for it, even if the manager often joked that the ball was bigger than him.

But over the years it had become clear that Lionel just wasn't growing. He was staying the same size, staying small.

It hadn't taken long for doctors to work out what was going on. Lionel had been diagnosed with a growth hormone deficiency. As a result, he had to inject himself with a growth hormone pretty much every day. It was a bit of a chore, but he'd got used to the routine of putting a needle into his leg. Plus he did enjoy seeing how watching the needle go in freaked his team-mates out.

Even though the treatment was going well, it was expensive, and Lionel's father, Jorge, could only afford to pay for two years of treatment. Lionel was going to need much more than that.

Newell's were desperate to help, but they couldn't

afford – or justify – paying for it, not for a twelve-year-old kid in their youth academy.

Lionel's mum and dad were working hard to support his career, but he knew that ultimately his height might be against him. It might be the one thing that stopped his football career before it had even started.

"Well, today we'll take you as you are, Leo," Franco said, as the three boys looked at the opposition team warming up. "We've got a final to win."

The Machine of '87 had travelled to Buenos Aires, Argentina's capital city, for a youth tournament, featuring the best teams from around the country.

So far, nobody in the tournament had slowed the machine down. Some of the teams that had taken them on had seemed daunted, almost scared, but the team they were playing now, in the final, seemed different.

"They look focused," Lionel muttered.

"Our first real test," Franco added.

"Huh! We've won every game without conceding – and you think *this* is going to be a test?" Sergio laughed. "Quique is half-asleep in goal most of the time! The real question is how many we'll score."

Lionel laughed. He had to agree with Sergio. So far at the tournament, Newell's had won their games 10-0, 7-0 and 5-0.

"Anything less than three or four and we should be embarrassed," Sergio joked.

As soon as the match began, it became clear that, focused or not, the opposition weren't a match for Newell's. They were physical and nipped at Lionel's heels, but he was too quick for them.

On an attack down the right wing, Lionel exchanged passes with Sergio before flicking the ball around a defender.

Lionel cut onto his left foot, then back onto his right, leaving another defender on the turf. As the keeper closed him down, Lionel lifted the ball over the keeper's head and watched it bounce over the line into the goal.

"I told you!" Sergio shouted. "Three or four, guaranteed!"

Newell's began to put on a show for the crowd that had come to see them. Lionel pulled out some of his favourite tricks, including the sombrero, where he flicked the ball over the head of a defender, before running around him.

They quickly added more goals, and by the time the full-time whistle went, Sergio had been proved wrong. They hadn't just scored three or four – they'd won the final 5-0.

With a winner's medal around his neck, Lionel wandered over to his dad, who'd been watching from the sidelines.

Over the past few months, Jorge's face had borne a permanent look of worry about Lionel's treatment and how he was going to pay for it.

But now a wide grin was plastered across his face.

"What's going on?" Lionel asked.

"I've just heard from my relatives in Spain. How do you fancy playing for Barcelona?"

4
THE NAPKIN CONTRACT

14th December, 2000
Pompeya Tennis Club, Barcelona, Spain

"The guy you want to impress is over there," Horacio Gaggioli, an agent who worked with Barcelona, told Lionel. He pointed to an older man standing at the side of the pitch.

"His name is Charly Rexach," Horacio continued. "He's my boss – and one of the sporting directors at Barca. If you get him on your side, you won't have any problems."

Lionel nodded as he felt his heart rate increase. He'd travelled a very long way to Spain for this trial with Barcelona. If they rejected him, he'd have to go back to Argentina. Surely that would mean the end of any football career.

But Lionel didn't need to worry – Gaggioli was on his side. He'd been impressed by the young Argentinian and had pushed for the transfer to happen. He'd even arranged for the club to pay for Lionel's growth hormone treatment.

And today, just after his thirteenth birthday, Lionel was taking part in a trial match with Barcelona's youth team.

Lionel's first touch of the game was sloppy, and the ball skipped under his boot. He looked over at Rexach, trying to read his expression.

"Don't look at him, focus on your football, Leo!" his dad shouted. The moment reminded Lionel of when he'd messed up his first touch that first time he'd played with Matias and Rodrigo. He needed to stop overthinking things and just do what he did best – play football.

The next time the ball came his way, he delicately controlled it. Arriving at the edge of the penalty area, he flicked the ball round a defender. Twisting his way past more challenges, he chipped the ball across the box, finding a striker who crashed home a header.

After the goal celebrations, Lionel glanced over at Rexach again. Just a moment ago, he'd been walking around the pitch to watch another game, but now he'd stopped to watch Lionel.

When the game ended, Lionel fell to his knees, exhausted. He'd given everything on the pitch and had played the best football of his life. He told himself if that wasn't enough to persuade Barcelona to sign him, then so be it. He could do no more.

Gaggioli and Jorge were standing together and they smiled as Lionel walked over to them.

"Your grandmother would be so proud of you," Jorge said, pulling him in for a hug. It had been a couple of years since Lionel's grandmother had passed away, and he still missed her. He wanted to achieve as much as he could in his football career, for her.

"Have I done enough?" Lionel asked Gaggiolo nervously.

"I think so," the agent replied with a smile.

Over the next few days, Lionel and his dad waited for the club to contact them. Eventually, a call came from Charly Rexach. He wanted to meet Lionel, Jorge and Gaggioli at a tennis club in Barcelona.

"The club are nervous," Rexach told them. "It's rare to sign a young guy like this from a country outside Europe."

"There's other clubs that will sign him if you don't," Jorge replied. "We can't stay like this forever."

"I know, I know," Rexach said, holding his hands up.

"We need something concrete or we're heading back to Argentina," Jorge added, politely but firmly.

There was a moment of silence as everyone looked at Rexach, waiting to hear what he would say.

"OK, how about this?" Rexach sighed. He pulled a pen out of his pocket, grabbed a napkin from a nearby table and began writing on it.

"This is a contract, OK?" he said. "As good as a typed agreement. We have witnesses here," he said, looking at Gaggioli.

"What does it say?" Jorge asked.

"Read it yourself," Rexach said, passing the napkin over to him. "It says that Leo is a Barcelona player. How's that for something concrete?"

"Really? That's it?" Lionel blurted in excitement.

"It's official, Leo," Jorge said, after looking at the napkin. "You're a Barca player!"

Lionel and his dad grabbed each other and hugged. Lionel's future – and the problem of paying for his growth hormone treatment – was now secure. Jorge breathed a sigh of relief.

"Thank you!" Lionel said, turning to Rexach and Gaggioli.

Rexach grinned. "This city is your new home," he said. "Make everyone in it proud of Barcelona's newest star."

"It's early days, Charly," Gaggioli said cautiously. "He's only a youth player!"

"Before long, everyone will know the name Lionel Messi," Rexach said, giving Lionel a wink. "See you at the training ground!" he added, as he got up and walked away.

5
THE MAN IN THE MASK

May 2003, La Masia Academy, Barcelona, Spain
Under-15 Copa Catalunya Final, Barcelona v Espanyol

"Are you really going to wear that thing?" Cesc Fàbregas asked Lionel, pointing at the mask lying next to him on the bench. "You won't be able to see a thing."

"I've got to," Lionel shrugged. "They won't let me play otherwise."

Only a week earlier, Lionel had fractured his cheekbone in the derby game against Espanyol,

Barcelona's biggest rivals. The doctors had told him the only way they'd let him play in today's final was if he wore the mask.

After signing for Barca, it had taken Lionel longer than he'd expected to settle into life in Spain. Because of registration issues, he was only allowed to play in friendlies and cup games at first, which made it difficult to build friendships with the other players.

At first, Lionel's family had moved from Argentina to Spain to be with him, but after a year his mum and his brothers had moved back to Rosario. He still had his dad with him but, even so, he felt lonelier than ever.

For a young player, joining a new club was always a big change. Lionel had joined a new club – *and* moved to a new city, in a new country on a new continent, thousands of miles from home.

"Don't worry," Jorge told him. "I know you're finding it hard, but as soon as you're allowed to play for the club properly, you'll make great friends with your team-mates, I'm sure of it. Either way, I'll always be here for you."

Jorge was soon proved right. The registration issue

was solved for Lionel's second season with the club and he soon became good friends with team-mates Cesc Fàbregas and Gerard Piqué.

The three of them were key players in what was being called Barca's greatest ever youth team, the "Baby Dream Team". Just as at Newell's Old Boys, Lionel found himself part of a golden generation of players at a club. They were sweeping everyone else aside, winning games 10-0, 6-0 and even one game 22-0.

"We've won it all if we win this match," Lionel said to Cesc.

"I think so," Cesc shrugged. "But this might be our last match together."

"What do you mean? We can move up the age groups. We'll be in the first team together soon."

"*You* might, Leo," Cesc smiled, "but I'm not going to take Xavi or Iniesta's place. It will be ages before I get through the B team."

"Well, I might not get picked over Ronaldinho," Lionel laughed. "So we'll play for the B team together."

"They'll find room for you *and* Ronaldinho," Cesc replied. "Anyway, I'm just being realistic. And I've already agreed a deal. I'm going to England, to Arsenal."

"What? Why Arsenal?" Lionel was stunned. He couldn't believe what he was hearing.

"They said I can train with the first team, even though I'm only sixteen. I'd be crazy to say no to that. You should think about it too."

Lionel shrugged. Over the years he'd been approached by a number of clubs, including the likes of Arsenal and Real Madrid, but he'd always imagined he'd start and finish his career at Barcelona. He couldn't imagine playing anywhere else.

"What's going on?" Gerard asked, sitting down next to Lionel.

"You won't believe this. Cesc is going to Arsenal. This might be our last game together."

"Ah," Gerard replied, avoiding eye contact with Lionel.

"You're not going as well, are you?" Lionel asked, suddenly feeling devastated.

"Well … nothing official. But I've spoken to Man United and I might go for it."

Lionel didn't reply. His two closest friends were both heading to England and he was going to be left here, on his own. He felt tears welling up in his eyes, but he blinked them away.

"Fine," he snapped. "You guys can enjoy England and the rain later. But today, we've got a final to win."

He picked up the mask and pulled it on, glad that now they couldn't see the upset in his eyes.

Unfortunately he quickly found that the mask was a huge disadvantage on the pitch. He could barely see a thing.

"I'm taking this off!" he shouted to Victor Vazquez, ripping the mask off and jogging to the touchline.

The coach, Álex García, quickly came over to him.

"You've got to keep that on, Leo," he shouted. "I can't let you play otherwise."

"I'll come off at half-time," Lionel replied. "I can't play in that mask. I promise you, nothing will happen."

A moment after taking the mask off, Lionel opened the scoring. A brilliant ball from Cesc found him, and he had the simplest of tasks to poke it past the keeper.

His second goal was all Leo. He picked the ball up

on the left, before dribbling infield, riding the strong challenges of the Espanyol defence.

He flicked the ball through the legs of one defender, skipped around another, and finally drove the ball hard from just inside the box into the bottom corner.

"Come on!" he shouted, jumping into the arms of his team-mates. "Are you still sure you want to leave?" he asked, looking at Cesc.

Cesc didn't reply.

After scoring two goals inside ten minutes, Lionel came off at half-time as promised, but Barca were already 3-0 up and the Cup was all but sealed.

As he sat on the bench, watching the second half play out, Lionel knew one thing for certain. Cesc and Gerard might leave, but he was going to stay. He hadn't felt this comfortable somewhere since he'd been at Newell's Old Boys.

He didn't want to start over again at a new place. He was going to make it work at Barcelona. This was where he belonged.

6
FIRST GOAL

May 2005, Camp Nou, Barcelona, Spain
Barcelona v Albacete

"I don't get it. Everyone can see I'm playing really well in training. Why haven't I been in the squad?"

"The boss is just easing you in, Leo. You're still so young," Andrés Iniesta replied. "We're in a title race and he doesn't want to take risks."

"I'm not a risk, though," Lionel protested. "I can make a difference."

After Cesc and Gerard had left Barca, Lionel had risen through the ranks. In less than a year he'd played for the under-17s, the under-18s, the C and the B teams, and he was soon part of the first-team squad, alongside the likes of Samuel Eto'o and Xavi.

Lionel had shocked the coaches and players alike, with his quick footwork and his dribbling skills, particularly his urge to head straight towards goal.

This was in sharp contrast to Barcelona's number 10 and their best player, Ronaldinho. He would frequently pull out tricks and flicks in the middle of the pitch a long way from goal, often for the entertainment and amusement of the crowd and his team-mates, rather than with any real intention.

Despite the differences in their styles, Ronaldinho had quickly taken Lionel under his wing.

"You've got good feet, Leo," Ronaldinho told him. "I think me and you could make an impact. Me on the left, cutting inside. You on the right."

"I like to be on the left," Lionel replied. "I mean, I'm left-footed."

"I know you are," Ronaldinho replied. "That's why

you should be on the right. Don't you want to cut inside and shoot? Try something crazy from long range? Score the goal of the season?"

"I just want the ball to go in," Lionel shrugged. "If I can play on the left, I've got a better chance of getting a good cross in, creating a goal."

"Trust me, Leo," Ronaldinho insisted. "You need to be on the right."

After hesitating to play Lionel because of his inexperience, the Barca manager Frank Rijkaard eventually gave Lionel his debut against Espanyol in October 2004.

At the age of 17 years, three months and 22 days, Lionel became the youngest player ever to play for Barcelona, in any competition. Lionel knew that if he was good enough for the first team at that age, there was no telling how far he could go.

But then, following his debut, and with Barca still in the hunt for the La Liga title, Rijkaard didn't play Lionel for months. Then came a game against bottom-of-the-table Albacete, and Rijkaard felt confident enough to give Lionel a chance in the squad.

"You nervous then, Leo?" Xavi asked him in the dressing room before the match.

"Nah. I've made my debut already. I'm ready to score my first goal," Lionel replied, watching Xavi's face break into a broad grin.

It looked to all the world that Barcelona were going to run out comfortable winners, but the match turned out to be much tougher than expected.

Lionel started on the bench. It was a tense first hour as Albacete held on at 0-0, but after 66 minutes Samuel Eto'o made the breakthrough to put Barca ahead.

"The floodgates will open now," Fernando Navarro, sitting next to Lionel on the bench, told him.

"I'm not so sure," Lionel replied. Albacete were defending well and even looked dangerous on the counter-attack.

The Camp Nou crowd were starting to get restless and there were groans of frustration every time a Barcelona attack broke down or a pass went astray.

"Leo!" Rijkaard shouted towards the bench.

"Me?" Lionel said, looking round to see if the manager was speaking to someone else.

"Who else here is called Leo? You're on. There's only a couple of minutes left, so keep the ball and don't do anything stupid."

"Let's get you that goal, then," Ronaldinho said, as Lionel came over to him.

A minute later, he got that chance from a brilliant Ronaldinho pass. The keeper came out and Lionel lifted the ball over him and into the back of the net.

He turned to celebrate, but caught something in the corner of his eye. The linesman standing at the side of the pitch had his flag raised. The goal was offside.

Lionel groaned. He was so sure he'd timed his run perfectly.

"Next time, bro," Ronaldinho chuckled, clapping him on the back. "We'll get you one they can't rule out."

As it turned out, "next time" was only a few moments later. Ronaldinho was once more at the centre of it, picking the ball up in midfield. The defenders were drawn to him, giving Lionel some space.

Ronaldinho lifted the ball over their heads and into Lionel's path. The ball bounced and Lionel spotted the keeper rushing out. He didn't need a touch this time and, exactly as before, he lifted it over the keeper's head, where it bounced over the line.

Lionel looked over to the linesman. This time there was no flag – the goal stood.

Lionel had his first Barca goal, his first professional goal!

He wheeled away in celebration, not quite sure where to turn or who to look at. Then he was quickly mobbed by his team-mates, with Ronaldinho lifting him up and placing him on his shoulders.

Hearing 90,000 fans in the Camp Nou cheering was the best feeling in the world, one he knew he was going to have again and again.

He was going to give Rijkaard no choice. The manager was going to have to play him.

7

ON THE GLOBAL STAGE

June 2006, FIFA WM-Stadion Gelsenkirchen, Germany
Argentina v Serbia and Montenegro

"The World Cup is next year, Leo. I think you can help us win it," Sergio Agüero told him during the first training session with the senior Argentina squad.

"There's no way I'll be part of that squad," Lionel replied, shaking his head. "I'm not even 18 yet."

Even though Lionel was still frustrated with his lack of game time at Barcelona, his efforts hadn't gone unnoticed. He'd been included in the Argentina squad for the 2005 World Youth Championship, going on to finish as the tournament's top scorer and winning the Golden Ball for best player.

That had earned him his first call-up to the Argentina senior side, but his debut had quickly turned from a dream into a nightmare when he'd been sent off only a couple of minutes after coming on.

He'd caught a defender in the face with his arm. It had been completely unintentional, but the referee had thought otherwise and had given Lionel a straight red card. He'd spent the rest of the match in the dressing room, crying by himself. The dream start to his international career had ended in the worst possible way.

Fortunately, the Argentina manager José Pékerman was forgiving. He knew Lionel had been unlucky and he was willing to give him a second chance.

His second debut came a month later, in a World Cup qualifying game against Paraguay.

This time he played the full game and he was able to impress, skipping past challenges, creating chances and even coming close to scoring.

"After that performance, you'll definitely be in the World Cup squad," Javier Mascherano told Lionel after the game.

Lionel didn't want to get ahead of himself, but he was starting to establish himself in the Barcelona first team as well, playing on the right wing, creating a ruthless front three with Ronaldinho and Samuel Eto'o. They quickly tore through every team in La Liga and were even ripping through European opposition in the Champions League.

They made it all the way to the Champions League final in Paris, but there was bad news. Lionel had torn his hamstring and had to miss the final.

He wasn't even in the city as Barcelona beat Arsenal 2-1 to lift the trophy.

"How come you weren't there?" Ronaldinho kept asking him. "You missed the celebrations. You didn't get your medal."

"I wasn't part of it."

Lionel had already begun to regret that decision, but it would just have been too painful, too hard, to be part of the celebrations for a final he didn't play in.

The biggest question on his mind now was, would he make the World Cup? It was a tense wait, but the call that Lionel had been waiting for soon arrived.

"Leo?"

"Yes, boss?"

"You're in the squad. See you at training camp."

Lionel had his phone on loudspeaker, so as soon as he hung up, he celebrated along with his family, who were all there to hear the news. He would be part of the squad. He would be going to the World Cup in Germany.

"I can't believe my son is going to be Argentina's newest World Cup scorer!"

"Give me a chance, Mum!" Lionel replied, but deep down, he knew he was going to score.

He spent the first game, against the Ivory Coast, as an unused substitute, but Pékerman had promised him a role in the next game – even if it was brief.

The next game was against Serbia and Montenegro and it was a must-win for Argentina if they were going to top their group.

The Serbs were a tough team, but Argentina quickly

took control, with a brace from Maxi Rodríguez and another from Cambiasso. With Argentina 3-0 up and with 15 minutes left, Lionel got his moment.

"On you go, Leo. Go and grab your first World Cup goal," Pékerman told him. "Make them forget Maradona."

Lionel was quickly into the thick of things. First he was taken out by a Serbian defender after skipping past him. Then he got the ball on the left-hand side and sprinted towards the box. He thought about the shot but spotted Hernán Crespo on the other side.

He slid a ball across and Crespo slammed it into the back of the net. 4-0!

But Lionel wasn't done yet. He wanted a goal.

Carlos Tevez added a fifth and then, with only a few minutes left to play, he slipped the ball into Lionel. It came onto his right foot, his weaker one, but he still knew what he was going to do. He took it into his stride easily and then drilled it hard past the keeper.

Lionel punched the air as thousands of Argentinians celebrated their newest superstar.

"Let's go, Leo!" Hernán Crespo shouted. "If you're

scoring in the World Cup now, who knows how many more you're gonna get."

Although the goal didn't mean anything for the result, it meant everything to Lionel. He'd made his mark at the World Cup.

Now he just needed to help Argentina go on and win the whole tournament.

8
EL CLÁSICO

March 2007, Camp Nou, Barcelona, Spain
Barcelona v Real Madrid

"It's good to have you back, Leo," Andrés Iniesta said with a smile. "We've missed you."

Lionel had spent the summer so obsessed with Argentina and the World Cup, he'd forgotten that he had another season with Barcelona to look forward to. They were the defending champions both in Spain and in Europe, and the pressure was on.

Lionel was determined to prove himself. The one thing sometimes levelled at him was that he rarely scored, and when he did, it wasn't against the big sides. Critics said he only scored in games against lower ranked teams, often going missing in the big games.

The season started slowly for both Lionel and Barcelona, and in mid-November he'd suffered a fracture in his foot, ruling him out for several weeks.

Then he'd been marked out of the game in the Champions League as Barcelona had been dumped out by Liverpool in the Round of 16.

But there was no game bigger for Barcelona than the game tonight – El Clásico, Barcelona v Real Madrid.

Tonight was a real opportunity for Lionel to prove that he was a big-game player. He was determined to prove himself.

"I'm going to score tonight," he said, turning to Andrés. "I want more goals. Now's no better time to start."

"We could do with it, Leo," Andrés admitted.

Barca were top of the league, but they'd been struggling and hadn't been sweeping every team aside as in the past.

And Real Madrid weren't too far behind. A defeat today would let them back in.

Real Madrid took the lead early on, when Ruud van Nistelrooy curled in from long range. It was the worst possible start and Lionel gritted his teeth as Madrid celebrated. He was going to have to be the one to step up and turn the game around.

Five minutes later, the ball came to him in the box from an Eto'o pass. He was in acres of space and had the easiest job to open up his body and slide it into the far corner.

Goal! Lionel had pulled Barca level.

Eto'o jumped on his back during the celebrations. "Big-game players score big-game goals!" the Cameroonian shouted in his ear.

Eto'o was right. It wasn't just about the goal. It was about proving the critics wrong, proving that Lionel could score in the big games.

Only a couple of minutes later, Real Madrid were back in front. A mistake at the back got them a penalty and van Nistelrooy added his second.

But Barca were still fighting and before the half was

up they were back level. Ronaldinho danced his way into the box, skipping past the challenges before getting a shot away. The ball was palmed out but only as far as Lionel, who drove the ball high into the top of the net.

Now he had two!

"You've got to get a hat-trick now, Leo!" Ronaldinho laughed.

The game continued at the same frenetic pace and half-time was a welcome relief. It was a few minutes to take a breather and get some water, before it all kicked off again.

There were fewer goals in the second half and, whilst the pace was still hard, both teams were worried about losing. The score remained at 2-2 until Sergio Ramos headed home from a free kick, silencing the 90,000 Barca fans again.

"Would be a good time for you to get that hat-trick now, Leo," Ronaldinho joked.

"Then I need you to set me up again!" Lionel protested.

Slowly, time was ticking away. Lionel needed the ball.

Eventually, with only minutes left, Ronaldinho fed the ball into him. Lionel's first touch was perfect. He opened his body up and moved away from his marker.

He skipped past the challenge of Helguera and flew into the box. The ball was on his left foot now, just the way he liked it. He could see the goal in his eyeline and he knew exactly what he was going to do.

He struck it hard across the keeper and watched it hit the back of the net. That was the equaliser! That was his hat-trick!

"COME ON!" he roared, sprinting towards the corner and kissing the Barcelona badge on his shirt, before he was mobbed by his team-mates.

"Well, you told me you were going to score, but you didn't say you were going to score three!" Andrés said to Lionel as they hugged after the final whistle.

A hat-trick in El Clásico. That was one for the critics, thought Lionel, the people who said he didn't score enough goals in the big games.

Now he knew for sure – he was really taking off.

9
PEP'S REVOLUTION

May 2009, Ciutat Esportiva Joan Gamper, Barcelona, Spain

"Another win today, then?" Lionel asked Gerard Piqué at the club's training ground. Lionel's childhood friend had just re-joined Barcelona from Man United and it felt good to have him back.

"Probably, but we can't take any chances. Playing Real Madrid won't be like the days of our youth team," Gerard replied.

"Honestly, I didn't think we'd do this well," Lionel admitted. "I mean, this is Pep's first real managerial job."

"Nobody did," Gerard nodded, "but Pep's been the best thing that's happened to this club since Cruyff."

"You think so?" Lionel replied, raising an eyebrow. Johan Cruyff was Barcelona's biggest legend, as a former player and manager. Pep Guardiola was another former Barcelona player and it wasn't too surprising that he was being compared to Cruyff.

Lionel had lost the 2007 Copa América with Argentina, but his impressive performances had led to him being named young player of the tournament. He'd then gone on to win a gold medal at the Olympic Games in 2008.

"Come on, Leo!" a voice called from outside the dressing room. "We need to do your warm-ups!"

It was the voice of Juanjo Brau, Barcelona's physio – and also Lionel's personal chaperone, nutritionist, coach, and now very good friend. He'd taken on all of these roles over the summer of 2008, the summer that had changed so much for Leo.

As he followed the physio out of the dressing room, Lionel thought about last season, the last year with Frank Rijkaard in charge. It had been one of the toughest years of his career so far.

He remembered the frustration and the disappointment as he'd pulled up clutching at his hamstring in a crucial Champions League game against Celtic. It had been his seventh different injury in the space of two years and would rule him out for several weeks.

Over his time in those two years, Lionel had rarely been fit for even 40 games in the season. Tonight would be his 47th game of this year, and there were still plenty left if Barca were going to go all the way in the Champions League and the Copa del Rey, as he felt they would.

"You taken your vitamins today, Leo?" Juanjo asked as they stepped out onto the pitch.

Lionel nodded.

"We're just going to start with stretches," Juanjo continued, "keep everything loose."

Lionel had begun working with Juanjo not long after Pep had taken over in the summer. Pep had been concerned about Lionel's lifestyle, his diet and his sleep regime. Lionel had taken to watching Argentine football late at night, and eating only rich meats at a local Argentinian steak house.

It had reminded him of home, and he'd taken comfort in the food, even if he knew it wasn't the best for him. He'd also spent a lot of time with Ronaldinho and Deco, who would often party late into the night after a game.

Pep had been keen to put a stop to all that. It might have worked for them a few years ago, but football had been changing. And Barcelona were falling behind.

Pep had sold the Brazilian players, including Ronaldinho, who only a few years previously had been a Ballon D'or winner.

But he'd kept Lionel. He believed there were big things to come from the little Argentinian.

"You're my star player, Leo," Pep had told him in the pair's first meeting. "I'm going to build this team around you. If you listen to me and follow my instructions, you're going to be better than Ronaldinho. You're going to be the best in the world."

Just like Grandma told me, Lionel thought to himself. Pep even gave Lionel the number 10 shirt that had been vacated by Ronaldinho.

Pep set Lionel a strict new diet and exercise regime too – no more late nights, no more steaks. Now it was fish and vegetables and getting eight hours of sleep.

Pep also told Juanjo to stick with Lionel, wherever he went. At first, it was tough for Lionel, feeling as if he was being watched all the time, but the results spoke for themselves. After struggling under Rijkaard to play 40 games in a season because of injuries, Lionel hadn't been injured at all under Pep.

And he'd scored over 30 goals in 46 games, putting Barca on course for a historic treble.

A win against Real Madrid tonight would put them within touching distance of a La Liga title.

The game started badly when Gonzalo Higuaín, Lionel's international team-mate, headed Real Madrid in front. But it didn't take long for Barca to strike back.

Lionel picked the ball up in the middle of the pitch. He spotted the run of Thierry Henry down the left-hand side and delicately chipped the ball into his path. It was completely missed by Sergio Ramos and Henry guided it into the back of the net.

Barca were level.

Barca's captain, Carles Puyol, headed them in front not long after, and then Lionel had his moment.

He'd been playing down the middle instead of on the wing over the last few months, and he was lurking in between the two centre-backs when Xavi won the ball back, high up the pitch. Real Madrid were caught off guard and Lionel had acres of space to run into.

Casillas came out, spreading himself, but Lionel was too good. He'd been in this position so many times this season, and the outcome was always the same. With his left foot, he poked the ball past the outstretched leg of the Madrid keeper.

At 3-1, Barcelona were running away with it.

In the second half, Real Madrid pulled a goal back, and for a moment it looked as if the game was back on.

But then Henry scored his second. And then, with fifteen minutes left, Lionel got the ball and flicked it into Xavi. The Barca midfielder was able to spin and fire the ball back into Lionel.

Lionel was once more in on goal, closing in on Casillas. He opened his body up as if he was going to slide it into the far corner, but instead he fired it hard into the near corner of the goal.

Barcelona had five!

"That's definitely the title!" Piqué roared, as they celebrated.

A few moments later Piqué got *his* goal – Barcelona's sixth – and Lionel could only agree with him. That surely *was* the title.

Now they just needed to get the next two on the list.

10
THE TREBLE

May 2009, Stadio Olimpico, Rome, Italy
Champions League Final, Manchester United v Barcelona

"Two down, one to go," Piqué chimed, as the Barca players walked through the large corridors of the Stadio Olimpico towards the dressing room.

"Don't talk like that," Iniesta replied. "You'll jinx it."

"It won't impact the game, Andrés. It's only a joke," Piqué scoffed.

It had only been a few weeks since Barcelona had

smashed Real Madrid 6-2 on their own patch. In the games that followed, they had lifted the Copa del Rey, before sealing the title.

Now they had their eyes on the Champions League.

"Let's not get cocky," Carles Puyol interjected. "These guys won it last year. They're a good team."

"You don't need to tell me," Piqué replied. "I was there."

The opponents for the Champions League final were Piqué's former club, and current holders of the competition, Manchester United. They were the team to beat and they featured currently the best player in the world – Cristiano Ronaldo.

As the Barca players turned a corner, they spotted Ronaldo heading into the United dressing room. He was almost the exact opposite of Lionel in every way. He was tall, right-footed, good in the air and blessed with a powerful shot.

Lionel on the other hand was a more subtle finisher, a dribbler with a low centre of gravity, ideal for cutting onto his left foot. Yet it was he and Ronaldo who were the best two in the world right now.

After scoring 37 goals in all competitions at only 22 years of age, most pundits were touting Lionel for the 2009 Ballon d'Or, the award given to the best player in the world. Lionel felt that if he could seal the treble for Barca, he'd have one hand on the award.

"Maybe you two guys should just go and play one-on-one," Piqué joked. "That's what everyone thinks this game is about anyway. Messi versus Ronaldo."

They quickly filed into the dressing room, where Pep was waiting to give a little pre-match talk.

"Quickly, guys," he began. "Sit down, get settled."

He paused, allowing them to sit down, then stayed quiet for a moment longer, letting his silence hang in the air.

"We are so close now, guys," he said. "We've won so many games, some of them beautifully and some of them the hard way. Now this is the last one."

The players nodded. The Champions League was the biggest trophy in club football and it meant more for them to win it than La Liga or Copa del Rey. This was the one they wanted.

"After this, you can go on your holidays. Enjoy

yourselves. But for one more night I need you focused."

Pep paused again. "We don't have Dani Alves, but we have so many good players. We have the players to win this."

Pep held their attention for a moment longer, then allowed them to break away and get themselves changed. Then he approached Lionel.

"You're going down the middle today, OK Leo?" he said. "Remember what we discussed all this season. You wait for your moments, don't work hard chasing the ball. But when you get it – explosive!" Pep clapped his hands together.

"They will leave space in the middle there," he continued. "You can exploit, you can drive."

Lionel nodded. He had extra motivation for today's game, beyond just lifting the trophy and sealing the treble. Three years ago, he'd been injured when Barca had won the trophy in Paris. He'd always regretted being unavailable and he was determined to make up for it.

To raise the stakes even higher, Lionel was yet to score against an English side. That had been constantly levelled against him. The reason why he couldn't be the best in the world was because he'd never scored against an English team. He was intent on changing that tonight.

United were a hard-working side and for the first ten minutes they forced Barca back, keeping them at the edge of their own box. But Barca quickly got a foot on the ball and started playing the passes, dominating the possession.

And only a few seconds later, they struck. Samuel Eto'o weaved his way into the box on the right-hand side and poked the ball under Edwin van der Sar.

Barca had the lead.

In the first half, neither Lionel nor Cristiano Ronaldo had any decent chances. This might have been the match of Messi v Ronaldo, but so far neither of them had really been involved.

With the second half underway, Barca held a narrow lead, but they knew they needed a second goal.

A poor clearance from van der Sar fell at the feet of Puyol. He drove into the midfield and flicked the ball out to Samuel Eto'o.

United were leaving gaps in their defence as they pushed for an equaliser, so Lionel drifted into the space behind Rio Ferdinand, waiting for the ball.

Xavi received the ball on the right wing and Lionel put his hand in the air. He knew that if anyone could pick him out, it was Xavi.

Lionel twisted in the air as he jumped to stop the ball from flying over his head. He somehow managed to direct it over the keeper, into the far corner.

Now Barca had two.

Lionel put his hands in the air and looked into the sky. *This is for you, Grandma*, he thought to himself.

What's more, Lionel had scored against an English side now, and he might just have won them the Champions League!

His goal took the wind out of United's sails and they were unable to respond. Barca had sealed the game. They'd won the treble – and Lionel had been at the centre of it.

As he looked at the medal hanging around his neck, he couldn't help but think again of his grandma. She'd always believed he could become the best player in the world and now, after winning the treble, many other people thought so too.

A lot had changed in the last year and, with Pep at the helm, he knew things were only going to get better.

This was just the beginning.

II

FROM GREAT TO GREATEST

April 2010, Lionel's Home, Barcelona, Spain

"I helped you be the best in the world, Leo," Pep had told him. "You've scored so many goals, so many nice goals. So many scrappy goals. So many important goals."

Lionel had nodded.

"I think I can get you more."

"Really?"

"Yes, yes. I want you to become the best of all time.

There's so many records that could be yours. You're what – 22? You can win so much."

"What do I need to do?" Lionel had asked. He trusted Pep implicitly now. Pep had guided him to so many trophies and it was his advice that had got him to this position.

"Trust your instincts. I'll set the team up to make sure you get the ball. Then you do the rest."

Many of Lionel's 41 goals for club and country had helped Barcelona finish 2009 with six trophies. It was the best year of Lionel's career by far, but after his conversation with Pep, he knew that he could go to even greater heights.

Even though Barca were competing with Real Madrid at the top of La Liga, their real focus was on Europe. After Man United had failed last season to win two Champions Leagues in a row, Lionel knew it would be a huge statement if he could make Barca the first club to accomplish that feat.

Next up were Arsenal in the quarter-finals. The team that Lionel's old friend Cesc Fàbregas had been playing for.

Barca had drawn the first leg away at Arsenal 2-2, so there was still a lot of work to be done at the Camp Nou.

"Are you excited to be seeing Cesc again?" Piqué asked.

"He's injured," Lionel replied. "He won't be playing."

"That's a shame," Piqué shrugged. "But good for us – he's one of their best players."

"I can't believe you scored four goals against us in one match," Cesc said to Lionel on the phone, after the second leg.

"Maybe it wouldn't have happened if you'd been there to stop me," Lionel joked, but Cesc didn't respond.

"Are you unhappy at Arsenal?" Lionel continued.

"Not unhappy exactly. But we're not winning as many trophies as I thought we would."

"Hmm … Pep told me earlier in the season that he wanted to set the team up to keep getting me the ball. What if I ask the club to sign you to help do that?" Lionel asked.

"I'd love to come back to Barca one day," Cesc said, sounding more upbeat, "but I don't know how realistic that would be."

"You keep possession and you create chances, Cesc. You're exactly the kind of player that suits Barca. Let me see what I can do."

12
MOURINHO V GUARDIOLA

April 2011, Santiago Bernabéu Stadium, Madrid, Spain
Champions League Semi-Final Second Leg,
Real Madrid v Barcelona

"Match number three. Are we ready?" Dani Alves nodded at Lionel.

The atmosphere in the dressing room was tense and quiet as the players changed into their match kit.

"I can't believe we lost the last one," Lionel grumbled.

Tonight was Barca's third meeting with their arch-rivals Real Madrid in the space of just a couple of weeks. They had drawn in the league, although that hadn't been enough to stop Barca's march towards another title.

But they had lost in the Copa del Rey final, with Cristiano Ronaldo scoring the match-winning header.

"They're a different side since José turned up," Andrés Iniesta added.

"It's hard not to get annoyed," Piqué replied. "They're constantly kicking and nipping at our heels."

"You don't need to tell me," Lionel muttered.

He'd experienced teams under José Mourinho many times before in his career, most recently in the Champions League semi-finals last year, when José's Inter had knocked Barcelona out. He'd gone on to win the competition and the treble with Inter.

That had earned José the Real Madrid job, and he'd brought his energy and emotion with him, passing it on to his players.

"This is Messi v Ronaldo once more," Andrés chuckled. "But we know who always comes out on top."

"Except in the Copa del Rey last week," Pep suddenly interjected.

Lionel glanced up at the boss and thought he looked more serious than at any point over his three years as Barca's manager. Pep was worried about tonight.

"Last week this team beat us, guys," Pep continued. "They got under our skin, they fought us for every ball, pressed our every touch and they beat us."

"If the ref had been … " Piqué began, but Pep cut him off.

"They were better than us. They deserved to win that game. It's up to us to prove that we deserve to win this one."

Pep paused for a moment.

"They're going to be the same as they always are tonight, guys," he said. "They're going to be angry. They're going to be in your face, begging you to foul, to get wound up. You mustn't respond. You have to stay calm."

The players nodded, but a few of them still looked very tense.

"Let me get angry for you," Pep added. "I'm going to be angry, I'm going to be wild. But you must be calm, guys. Stay calm. Keep the ball and pass the ball. Just keep moving and passing. Don't worry about anything else."

Lionel nodded. He'd spent his whole life being kicked and pushed by people bigger than him. He'd learned not to respond. He'd learned simply to pick himself up and carry on. Show them what he could do with the ball.

Tonight would be no different.

The game was a tough and vicious midfield battle. It became clear that Real Madrid were looking to hold on for a 0-0 draw in the first leg. They weren't interested in pushing forward too much and it was going to be up to Barcelona to break them down.

Every time Lionel got the ball, he was quickly closed down by a whole huddle of white shirts, kicking and prodding at him. He would have to be at his very best to score tonight.

In the second half, the game changed. One of Lionel's closest markers, the Portuguese defender Pepe, was given a red card. Real were down to ten men.

Now Lionel had more time on the ball. He could get two or three touches before he was closed down. He could look up and pick out a pass.

He could see in the eyes of the Real Madrid players that they were tired. They had been working hard for 70 minutes and they couldn't do much more. Barca needed to strike.

Pep had sensed the same thing and threw on pacy winger Ibrahim Afellay. If he could create space down the right and get a cross in, Lionel would be ready.

Moments later, it happened. Afellay burst down the right-hand side, dodging Marcelo's challenge. Lionel knew exactly where the Dutch winger was going to put the ball and darted towards the near post.

The ball was fizzed into the box and Lionel was the first one there, diverting the ball home with his left foot.

Barcelona had got themselves a crucial away goal at the Bernabéu.

"Let's get a second," Lionel shouted, as his team-mates came to celebrate. "Let's get two."

"We only need one, boys," Xavi said. "We're a man up. Let's see this game out, don't take any risks."

For the next ten minutes they played the ball around, keeping hold of the ball and keeping Real Madrid at bay.

But Lionel wasn't satisfied. He wanted two.

He picked the ball up in the middle of the Real Madrid half and fed it to Sergio Busquets. Busquets waited until Lionel came round his marker, and then just flicked it back to him.

It was just Lionel now, in a sea of white shirts, just as it had been when he was a kid. He sprinted forward, leaving the first one in his wake.

He darted away from Sergio Ramos and then skipped over a challenge from Raúl Albiol. He was moving at some speed now as he sprinted into the box. He could see the goal opening up in front of him.

Marcelo came in from behind, while Ramos and Casillas came rushing towards him, but Lionel used his balance to divert the ball across goal with his weaker right foot as he tumbled over.

GOAL!

There were gasps from the home crowd as the ball rolled into the back of the net. It was an incredible solo goal and no other player in the world could have scored it.

"I told you," Iniesta said, as he hugged Lionel during the celebrations. "You always beat Ronaldo."

13

RECORD-BREAKER

December 2012, Benito Villamarín Stadium, Seville, Spain
Real Betis v Barcelona

"How many is the record again?" Cesc Fàbregas asked, leaning over towards Lionel. "What do you need?"

"One to tie it, two to break it," Lionel replied, a coy smile playing on his lips. It felt good to have his childhood friend back with him in the Barcelona dressing room.

Cesc had re-signed for the club in the summer of

2011, the summer after Barcelona had won yet another Champions League title, Lionel's third with the club. Lionel had also scored in that final, as they'd once more beaten a Manchester United side.

Last season, Lionel had broken more records than ever, finishing the season with an incredible 73 goals, breaking the European record for the most goals scored in a single season.

But despite Lionel's personal achievements, it had been a disappointing year for the club. Barca had lost their La Liga title to Real Madrid, they'd been beaten in the Champions League by Chelsea and, worst of all, Pep Guardiola had left.

The new manager was Pep's right-hand man and close friend Tito Vilanova. They were now half-way through the season and were flying at the top of La Liga. The results under Vilanova seemed to be speaking for themselves.

But that wasn't what Lionel was interested in tonight. He was after another record – one that had stood for over 40 years and was held by legendary German striker Gerd Müller. Müller had scored 85 goals over a single calendar year for club and country. Lionel currently stood on 84.

Many pundits thought that Müller's record would never be broken, but then again, they'd probably never thought that a player like Lionel would come along.

Betis were a tough team to play and Lionel felt his nerves tingling, nerves he hadn't felt in years. It hadn't sunk in before the game, but now he was standing on the pitch, he realised he was desperate to get the record. He needed this.

Luckily, he didn't have to wait too long to get the nerves out of his system. Just 15 minutes into the match, he picked the ball up on the edge of the box. He knew exactly what he was going to do. He had done it 84 times already this year.

Skipping past the challenges of the defenders and moving into the box, he drilled it hard with his left foot, dragging it across the keeper and into the far corner.

It had only taken him 15 minutes to get his 85th goal. Now he was level with Müller.

"Happy now? Right, Leo?" Iniesta said as they celebrated.

"I'm just level," Lionel replied. "I need to get another. I need to get the record."

It only took another ten minutes for Lionel to get his second. He'd been worried that he would go a long time without getting the record-breaking goal he needed, but now his nerves had settled.

Iniesta picked the ball up inside the box and backheeled it towards Lionel. He didn't take a touch, but instead just drilled it towards goal.

It was the same result as the first time, and it whistled across the ground and landed in the far corner.

He'd overtaken Gerd Müller. The name of Lionel Messi would now always be in the record books.

"On Sky Sports they said you need to prove you can win trophies without Pep," Cesc told him, after the game.

"I don't usually care what the papers say, but if I want to become the greatest of all time, I'll have to," Lionel replied. "Anyway, how do you like it at Barca? Glad I persuaded the club to sign you?"

"*I* am," Gerard Piqué interrupted. "The three amigos, all back together!" he said, as he put his arms around

Lionel and Cesc. "Who'd have thought we'd all be playing for the Barca senior team, back when we were playing in the youth team. It's what dreams are made of!"

"You know what will make that dream better? Winning trophies together!" Lionel replied with a grin.

14
MESSIDEPENDENCIA

May 2013, Camp Nou, Barcelona, Spain
Champions League Semi-Final Second Leg
Barcelona v Bayern Munich

"They're calling it *Messidependencia*," Lionel's brother Matias told him.

"What's that?" Lionel asked.

"Everything Barca do has to involve you at some point. It means they're going to struggle if you're not fit."

Although last season Barca had lost the La Liga title

to Real Madrid, this time around they were streaking away at the top of the table. Tito Vilanova had picked up where Pep had left off.

"Just look at the stats, Leo," Matias continued. "Last year you were involved in, what, a quarter of the goals? It's doubled since then."

"I don't look at the stats," Lionel laughed. "I'm just focused on the football. Anyway, let's not talk about it now. Tell me, how's the foundation work going?"

Matias and their mother managed the Leo Messi Foundation, back in Rosario. Lionel had established the foundation in 2007, after visiting a hospital for sick children in Boston. He'd set it up to improve healthcare, education and sport for children around the world.

"Yeah, it's all going really well. It's been hard to top that solid gold replica of your left foot though – the one we sold for five million dollars to raise money for the Tohoku earthquake victims in Japan," Matias said.

"That's such a crazy way to raise money," Lionel said, shaking his head. "But it's for a great cause, so – you know … "

"Yeah. Imagine if Grandma was here now, to see her

grandson win a record four Ballon d'Ors in a row, whilst raising huge sums for charity. She'd be *so* proud of you."

Nevertheless, Matias could still see problems on the horizon for Barca, even if Lionel didn't want to talk about it. Pep had wanted to build the team around his brother, to get him as much ball as possible. But maybe now it had gone too far.

Then, in April, disaster struck. Barcelona were away in the Champions League quarter-finals at PSG when, chasing a ball, Lionel pulled up. He stopped running and grabbed at the back of his leg, feeling pain like he hadn't felt in years. He knew it was his hamstring.

He missed the next few games, but then played another 45 minutes in the second leg to help Barcelona into the semis.

He missed another few league games with the injury, but returned to play 90 minutes in the first leg against Bayern Munich at the Allianz Arena. It was one of the worst days of his Barcelona career so far.

He could barely walk, let alone run, and every time he picked up the ball he was surrounded by a sea of red shirts. And for the first time in his life, he didn't have the acceleration to skip away from them. They would just take the ball off him.

He played the full 90 minutes as Barcelona were thrashed 4-0 by a Bayern team who completely outclassed them.

The papers were full of the Messidependencia stories that Matias had mentioned. With Lionel struggling with a hamstring injury, Barcelona looked weak going forward. It seemed as if Barcelona's tiki-taka style had been replaced by the relentless energy and pressing of Bayern.

The era of Barcelona was over.

And tonight, Lionel was sitting on the bench for the second leg. He'd tried all he could to get fit, to get himself back in shape for the match, but it hadn't been enough. He knew that if he was out on that pitch he would only be a liability for his team.

"Come on then, lads," Lionel said to himself on the bench as the game kicked off.

Four-nil down, Barca's players and fans knew that their chances of winning the tie were slim, but they could at least try to win the second leg to show the world that Barcelona weren't done yet. With Lionel on the bench, the rest of the team could put to bed all the Messidependencia rumours.

But it wasn't to be.

Lionel watched helplessly as Bayern ripped through the Barcelona team for the second time in a week. The Germans scored three goals in the second half, to record a massive 7-0 win on aggregate that shocked the football world. Barcelona were out of the Champions League at the semi-final stage once again.

For the first time in his life, Lionel was worried about the future of his career.

15
SO CLOSE

July 2014, Maracanã Stadium, Rio de Janeiro, Brazil
2014 World Cup Final, Germany v Argentina

"How're you feeling then, Leo?" Jorge asked his son. "You good?"

"I'm feeling fit – so I'm confident," Lionel replied calmly.

"There's no reason why you can't go all the way then!" Jorge replied with a smile. "Stay calm, stay focused, and you can win this. Just think! Bringing the

World Cup back to Argentina would really put you in the record books – again!"

"Don't say that! I don't need more pressure. Everybody is expecting me to beat Maradona's record."

"Don't worry about any of that," Jorge urged. "You're not Diego, you're Leo. Just be yourself."

Lionel smiled. Ever since the very beginning – from that first game at the age of five, when he'd just made up the numbers for his brothers' team, right up to his current World Cup preparations – his dad had been with him all the way.

Jorge took his role as father very seriously, but he was much more than just a dad. He was Lionel's agent, his support, his friend – and his coach. Lionel knew that if he'd had to go on his journey alone, he wouldn't have achieved anywhere near as much.

Barca's season had been disappointing. Despite signing Neymar for £49 million, Tito Vilanova had left the club because of illness. Gerardo Martino, another product of Newell's Old Boys back in Rosario, had replaced him, but he'd struggled to deliver results.

Barca only finished second in the league and had

been struggling in Europe. They were going to end the season without any serious silverware.

But whilst he'd never admit it, that wasn't what Lionel was really aiming for. For the last few years he'd been looking at the World Cup.

He was the captain of his country now and he knew they were in the best position ever to go on and win the tournament.

Despite what he'd said to his dad, he knew that this was his opportunity to equal Maradona's achievements and cement himself as the best player in Argentinian history – and of all time.

For the first time in decades the tournament was being held in South America, and Lionel knew there would be many Argentinian fans at the games. He'd even paid for many of his family and friends in Argentina to attend his matches.

He scored four times in the group stage to lead Argentina to the top of their group. Three hard games followed, with Argentina getting tight wins in all of them to get through to the final.

They'd expected to face arch-rivals Brazil in the

final, but the hosts had been thrashed 7-1 by Germany in their semi-final.

"Who'd have thought we'd get here, huh?" Sergio Agüero asked, looking at Lionel across the dressing room. "When we were in the youth teams, all those years ago?"

"*I* did," Lionel replied. "We were the best in the world then. Why shouldn't we be now?"

He was trying to appear more relaxed than he felt, but he couldn't quite do it. He knew that Sergio must be feeling equally nervous.

For all that, Argentina had the squad to do it. They had two of the best strikers in the world in Sergio Agüero and Gonzalo Higuaín. They had some of the best playmakers in the world, a title-winning full-back in Pablo Zabaleta and a world-class defensive midfielder in Javier Mascherano.

"OK lads, we know Germany's threats," Lionel added, taking on his role as captain. "But we know their weaknesses too. They'll want a fast start, blow us away like they did with Brazil. But if we weather that, then there's gaps to exploit."

"They play a high line," Mascherano added. "There's plenty of space in behind, so if we can time our runs, we'll get through."

"They also conceded twice against Ghana," Lionel reminded them. "And almost lost to Algeria in the last 16. They're not invincible. Don't be fooled because they won the semi by so much."

It was almost time to go out onto the pitch. Lionel knew he should say a few words as the captain, but he didn't know what to say. He'd always led by example on the pitch, not by being vocal in the dressing room.

"I shouldn't have to motivate you for this one, guys," he said. "It's the World Cup final. This is it. One shot to make history, to become legends. We *will* get chances tonight. We just have to make sure we take them."

In the blink of an eye, they were out of the dressing room and on the pitch.

It was a cagey start to the game, with both teams unwilling to take any chances and push on. But after 23 minutes, the biggest chance fell to Argentina. A miscued header from Toni Kroos fell at the feet of Higuaín. He had nobody around him and was unmarked as he burst in on goal. But the striker was nervous, and his shot flew well wide of the goal.

The best chance of the match had come for Argentina, but now it was gone.

Just before half-time, Germany had their moment with a crashing Benedikt Höwedes header, bouncing off the post and then into the arms of Sergio Romero in goal. It was still 0-0.

Early in the second half, Lionel got his chance. The ball was fed into him and he spun away from Boateng, bearing down on goal from the left-hand side. He knew exactly where he was going to put the ball as he struck it with his left foot, aiming for the far corner.

But as he watched, the ball missed the far corner and trickled just wide of the post. It was still 0-0.

Chances came and went for both teams for the rest of the second half, but at the full-time whistle it was still goalless. Extra time now loomed.

Both teams were exhausted and struggled to make any impact on the game in the final thirty minutes. But then Germany struck. Mario Götze chested a cross and volleyed it into the top corner.

Argentina were staring down the barrel of a final defeat. Lionel had one last chance with a free kick in the final minute, but it was too far out and he couldn't generate the accuracy.

The game was done. Germany had won the World Cup. Argentina, and Lionel, had lost.

As he trudged up the steps to collect his runners-up medal, Lionel glanced longingly at the World Cup trophy.

He would be returning to Barcelona empty-handed. And he couldn't be sure he'd ever get the chance with Argentina again.

16
REVENGE

May 2015, Camp Nou, Barcelona, Spain
Champions League Semi-Final, Barcelona v Bayern Munich

"This is our chance for revenge, Leo," Javier Mascherano said, fixing Lionel with an intense look.

"I saw his press conference from the other day," Neymar added. "He says he knows how to stop you."

The man they were talking about was, of course, Bayern and Germany keeper Manuel Neuer. The man who had robbed Argentina of the World Cup last summer, the man who'd been in goal at Lionel's worst Barcelona moment, the 7-0 aggregate thrashing just two years ago.

After the World Cup, it was another summer of change at Barcelona. Coach Gerardo Martino had been replaced by former Barca midfielder Luis Enrique, who'd made a number of changes, selling Cesc Fàbregas and Alexis Sánchez, and bringing in Luis Suárez, Ivan Rakitić and Marc-André ter Stegen.

"Football has moved on," Enrique told the players in his first meeting with the team. "Tiki-taka. It was great, it was beautiful, but we saw at the World Cup and against Bayern that we need more intensity."

After a slow start, Barcelona kicked into gear. The manager moved Lionel onto the right wing, Neymar onto the left and new striker Luis Suárez down the middle. Together, they formed the MSN trio that was tearing teams apart across Spain and Europe.

In May, Barca were only a couple of wins away from the La Liga title, a competition in which Lionel was now the all-time record goalscorer. But today they had a Champions League semi-final.

For the second time in three years, Barca were up against Bayern and had a chance to take revenge for their humiliating 7-0 loss in 2013.

But now, Bayern were managed by none other than Pep Guardiola. Just as he'd done at Barca, Pep had immediately transformed Bayern into a winning machine, and Lionel knew they were going to be tough to stop.

"It's going to be really weird facing Pep," Lionel said.

"Have you seen their team? It looks like a back three," Gerard Piqué replied.

"Never mind that, what about Lewandowski?" Dani Alves asked.

"I've shut down Cristiano Ronaldo," Gerard smirked. "I'm not worried about Lewandowski."

"We know they're going to play a high line," Lionel told Luis and Neymar before kick-off. "They'll take risks – Pep can't help himself. We have to strike when they're vulnerable."

Lionel flashed a smile at Pep in the tunnel, but he didn't want to talk to him and risk losing focus before the match. This was business.

In the first 15 minutes, the movement of the MSN trio pulled the back three of Bayern from side to side, but then, in typical Pep fashion, Guardiola reacted cleverly to what was happening in the game and changed his formation. The space for MSN to play in disappeared.

"Looks like he's taken a leaf out of Mourinho's book," Iniesta commented. "They're going for the 0-0."

For 78 minutes, it seemed as if Bayern were going to hold on for the 0-0, but then the slip up that MSN had been waiting for happened. The ball was given away by Bayern's left-back, Bernat, and Lionel found himself with the ball on the edge of the box.

The Bayern defenders were tired and didn't close him down. He flicked the ball onto his left foot and fired it towards goal. It bounced just in front of Neuer towards the right-hand post.

GOAL!

"COME ON!" Lionel roared as he sprinted towards the Barcelona fans. They were going just as crazy as he was. This was a goal that had been two years in the making.

"So much for him knowing how to stop you!" Neymar shouted.

"We need a second to kill the game off!" Lionel replied.

Three minutes later, he had an opportunity to get it. Rakitic´ fed the ball into Lionel on the right-hand side of Bayern's box. He dribbled into the box, luring Jerome Boateng towards his left foot, before shifting the ball the other way. Boateng was left sitting on the turf as Lionel skipped away.

Lionel stared down Neuer, the man who was supposed to stop him. The keeper made himself big while closing Lionel down, but Lionel knew exactly what he was going to do and he deftly chipped it over the keeper.

"That's world class, Leo!" Luis Suárez grinned, as he celebrated the goal with the other two members of the MSN trio. Just as against Real Madrid four years ago, Lionel had scored two crucial goals in a Champions League semi-final. And just like four years ago, Lionel was determined to go on and win the whole thing.

There was still time for more before the end. Lionel fizzed a pass into Neymar, who tucked it under Neuer to seal a massive 3-0 victory. Barcelona had been magnificent.

"People said we were done," Xavi said, gathering the team. "They said that Barcelona were on the way out. Well, we proved them wrong tonight. Barcelona are back!"

As Lionel was celebrating with his team-mates after the final whistle, he felt a hand on his shoulder. It was his former manager.

"Amazing performance, Leo. I'm glad you were on my team for so many years, when I didn't have to figure out how to stop you!" Pep said.

"Ha ha! Thanks, boss," Lionel replied. After everything they'd achieved together, Lionel thought it would feel wrong to call Guardiola anything else.

"Good luck in the final. You've been there before, you know what to do," Pep continued.

17
THIRD TIME LUCKY

June 2016, MetLife Stadium, New Jersey, USA

2016 Copa América Final, Argentina v Chile

"So we've got the treble," Luis Suárez joked with the other two members of Barca's MSN trio. "It's as if there's a trophy for each of us."

"We deserve all of them," Neymar replied. "We've been unstoppable this year."

Barca's MSN trio had helped the club finish the season with a La Liga, Copa del Rey and Champions

League treble, equalling the feat of Pep's Barca team in 2009.

But the previous summer, Lionel had lost his second Copa América final on penalties to Chile. It had been his second consecutive major final defeat with his country, and he'd been devastated.

"Why is it that Argentina keep getting to finals and losing them when I'm in the team?" Lionel asked his dad.

"You can't blame it on yourself, Leo. You can't control what everyone else does," Jorge replied. "You just need to believe that, if you keep your head down, an international trophy will eventually come your way."

This year, a special edition of the Copa América was being hosted in the USA, so instead of having to wait four years for another chance to win the competition, he only had to wait one.

It was his opportunity to right the wrongs of the previous year.

Argentina cruised through the group stage, thrashing Bolivia and Panama. In the quarter finals, they battered Venezuela and in the semis, they crushed hosts USA 4-0.

No doubt, they were the best team in the tournament. Lionel had five goals to his name, while Higuaín, Di María, Agüero, Ezequiel Lavezzi and Érik Lamela were all in the form of their lives. Éver Banega and Lucas Biglia were pulling the strings in midfield, while Nicolás Otamendi anchored their defence.

It felt like fate to Lionel that they had to play Chile in the final again, the team they'd lost to last year on penalties. It was the perfect opportunity for revenge.

Thousands of fans from Chile and Argentina made the trip to New Jersey for the match. The atmosphere was lively and Lionel wanted to channel the energy from the stands into his performance on the pitch.

"Good luck, Leo," Chile's captain, Claudio Bravo, also Lionel's Barca team-mate, said at the coin toss before the match. "If it was any other competition, I'd be cheering you on."

"Same to you," Lionel smiled back.

It wasn't typical of Lionel to feel nervous, but he could feel it in his body now. He needed this desperately. He couldn't finish his career without an international trophy and, at 29, he knew that time was running out.

From the start, chances were few and far between, but Argentina were slightly edging the game. Ángel Di María was everywhere in midfield and Lionel couldn't help but grin. They had missed him at the World Cup and it was crucial to have him back.

After only 30 minutes, Lionel was clattered by Marcelo Díaz, who was already on a booking.

"Ref!" Lionel shouted. "He's got to go! That's a second yellow!" The choice was out of the ref's hands. It was a clear second yellow card and Chile were down to ten men.

"We've got to make this count now, lads," Lionel said, turning to his team-mates. "We've got 60 minutes to get a goal. Let's do this!"

The game was bad tempered now, with tackles flying in from both sides. Lionel was certain he should have had a penalty, but instead he received a yellow card for diving. Even he wasn't above the atmosphere of the game as he wasted no time protesting to the ref.

Then, only 15 minutes after Díaz had been sent off, Marcos Rojo flew into the back of Arturo Vidal and the referee gave him a straight red card. Argentina's man advantage over Chile hadn't even lasted until half-time.

"We've got to calm down, guys," Lionel urged at half-time, but in the second half tempers remained high and challenges continued to fly.

Chances were still few and far between and, when they did come, they were skewed wide or blasted over. Nobody could keep a cool head and finish.

And then, just like a year ago, it went to penalties.

"We've got this, lads," Lionel insisted, gathering his team. "Stay calm, stay cool. Pick your spot and just hit it. Don't worry about the keeper. Don't worry about anything else. We've got this."

He was talking to himself as much as anyone else, and he prayed they couldn't see how nervous he was.

Chile were up first and quickly handed Argentina the advantage, when Vidal blasted straight at Romero in goal. Now it was Lionel, to set the tone for his team, to lead by example.

He took a short run up, avoiding eye contact with Bravo in the Chile goal. He sprinted forward, looking to curl it to his right and into the top corner.

But he got it all wrong. The ball sailed past Bravo

and then sailed over the bar. Lionel didn't see where it landed. He grabbed his shirt, looked down at the floor and screamed with anger.

He trudged back to his team, not daring to look at them. Agüero grabbed him in a hug.

"It's alright, Leo," he said. "There's plenty left. They missed as well, so it's still 0-0. We can still do this."

But Lionel didn't believe him. He just seemed destined to never win a trophy with his country. Why would that change now?

The rest of the shootout, he watched in a daze. Everyone scored until Lucas Biglia missed for Argentina. Then Lionel sank to the floor as Francisco Silva won it for Chile.

He had lost again. Three finals in three years.

As he stood for the third time in a row and watched another team celebrating, he turned to Agüero, shaking his head and wiping tears from his eyes.

"I can't do this again," he sobbed.

He was sure.

He'd never play for Argentina again.

18
RETIREMENT

July 2016, Lionel's family home, Rosario, Argentina

"You can't retire just because you've reached three finals in a row and lost them! You're so close, you can't give up now!" Matias urged Lionel.

"I thought you wanted to be the greatest. You're never going to be that without an international trophy," Rodrigo added.

After the disappointment of losing the Copa América

final, Lionel had stayed in South America to spend some time with his family, away from football.

Lionel had also made an announcement to the media that he was retiring from international football, but a campaign had started in Argentina to try to change his mind.

Lionel's family were trying to do the same.

"You're only 29, Leo. That's the peak of your career. Even the greats don't retire from international football at that age," Jorge told him. "You've got so much time left to win a tournament with Argentina, and it shows you're doing something right if you keep reaching finals. It's just a matter of time. Look how the fans reacted to your announcement. They know it too."

His family kept on reasoning with him.

"What do you think your grandma would say if she could hear you saying this?" Lionel's mum asked. "You know she'd say that you're crazy! She always knew before any of us – even you – that you'd be the best player in the world.

"She knew you as a fighter, Leo, and even though you've been knocked down, you have to keep getting up and fighting for what you want. If anyone can win an international trophy from here, it's you."

It took a while, but after a few days Lionel turned to his family and said, "OK, I'll do it. I'll keep going. I'm going to win a trophy with Argentina – and this time, nothing is going to stop me."

19
THE LAST MATCH

April, 2021 Estadio La Cartuja, Seville, Spain
Copa del Rey Final, Athletic Bilbao v Barcelona

Lionel had never expected it to come to this. He'd endured some hard and difficult lows in his career with Barcelona. He'd almost joined Inter Milan when he'd first broken through, and he'd had talks with Chelsea in 2014 after a difficult year.

But he'd never really expected to leave Barcelona – *ever*. Until, last season.

Following Argentina's loss against Chile in the 2016 Copa América final, the MSN era at Barcelona had quickly fallen apart. While Real Madrid won an incredible three Champions Leagues in a row, Luis Enrique left to be replaced by Ernesto Valverde, Neymar left for PSG and Iniesta moved to Japan.

Lionel had seen so many players and managers come and go during his time at Barca, but he'd always remained at the centre of it all, scoring around 50 goals a season, while trying to hold the team together.

After winning the league in the 2018/19 season, Barca were knocked out of the Champions League semi-finals against Liverpool, after being humiliated 4-0 at Anfield.

Then came the Champions League quarter-final. Barca took on Bayern Munich in a game held at a neutral venue in Lisbon. A one-off knockout tie, the winner would go on to the semis.

The match quickly turned into a humiliation as Bayern ran riot and thrashed Barcelona 8-2. It was the lowest point of Lionel's career and, for the first time, he asked to leave Barcelona.

There was huge interest from the likes of PSG and Man City, but none were able to cement a deal that both Lionel and Barca would agree to.

Barcelona were desperate to keep him, but as his contract was up the following year, there was little they could do.

Eventually, he agreed to stay for one more season. Barca brought in Ronald Koeman as manager and off-loaded a number of players, looking instead to promote from within, relying on the famous Barcelona youth system.

So, going into the final game of the season – the Copa del Rey final against Athletic Bilbao – Lionel genuinely didn't know if he was staying or going. There was a very real possibility that this would be his last game for the club.

No fans were allowed in the stadium because of the coronavirus pandemic, but if Lionel was going to leave, he knew that he couldn't lose his last game at the club. He had to finish on a high.

As he walked into the stadium, he heard a familiar voice call him over.

"Leo, can I have a quick word?" It was the new club president, Joan Laporta. "I just wanted to say that, whether you end up staying or leaving, you have done more for this club than anyone could have dreamed. You've come a long way since signing that contract on a napkin!"

"I haven't thought about that for a long time," Lionel laughed, "but thank you. All I've done is try my best – and I guess it's mostly worked out."

"Let's end this season with a bang, alright lads?" Leo said, looking around the dressing room at some of the younger players – the likes of Pedri, Sergiño Dest and Óscar Mingueza.

"We get our hands on that trophy and we let them know that we'll be back next year. Barcelona aren't done yet."

Barca almost took the lead early on, with Frenkie de Jong hitting the post after Lionel had slipped the ball back to him. But Bilbao defended resolutely, and at half-time it was still 0-0.

Barcelona continued to press and, after several chances went wide, Antoine Griezmann blasted them in front after a free-flowing move. Minutes later, de Jong doubled their lead with a stooping header.

Then Lionel took over. If it was to be his last game for Barca, then he was going to put on a show for the fans watching at home.

He got the ball on the right, going through the gears as he moved into midfield and exchanged passes with de Jong. The final pass slipped Lionel into the box, and he effortlessly cut inside and passed the ball through the keeper with a stroke of his left foot.

Barcelona were 3-0 up and cruising. They were going to end the season with a trophy.

Moments later, Lionel got his second. Jordi Alba cut the ball back and he was there, running onto it to strike it past the keeper.

At full-time, as Lionel lifted the Copa del Rey trophy in front of an empty stadium, he just felt sadness. He had a feeling that this was the last trophy he'd win with Barcelona – and the fans hadn't even been here to see it.

Now he accepted that he was willing to say goodbye to the club that had given him so much joy, that had seen him go from a young kid to one of the best in the world.

He was ready for the next chapter.

20
NEW HORIZONS

September 2021, Parc des Princes, Paris, France
Paris-Saint Germain v Manchester City

"Just like the old days, eh?" Neymar grinned as he and Lionel walked out onto the pitch in front of the lively Parisian crowd.

After the toxic atmosphere that had consumed Barcelona in Lionel's last couple of years there, PSG almost seemed like a blessed relief. It was a bonus too that he was reunited with his friend, Neymar.

Fans were back in the stadium now after the pandemic, and Lionel was happy to hear the boisterous crowd optimistic about the match ahead, rather than worrying about how many goals they were going to lose by.

There was a core of top-quality players in the team, including Kylian Mbappé, Ángel Di María, Marquinhos, Achraf Hakimi and Neymar himself. It was a squad set up to compete for the major trophies, both in France and in Europe.

Despite the pain and the disappointment of leaving Barcelona in the way he had, Lionel too was excited. This was an opportunity to put to bed the critics who claimed he could only do it within the system at Barcelona.

It was an opportunity too finally to get his hands back on the Champions League trophy – something that was not going to happen at Barcelona anytime soon.

After an injury-hit start to the season, Lionel's first chance came in the Champions League. PSG had been drawn in the same group as Pep Guardiola's Manchester City.

It was a chance to see Mbappé, Neymar and Lionel playing together for the first time. It was a chance too for PSG to send a clear message to the rest of Europe, by beating one of the best teams around.

PSG took the lead after just seven minutes, and in a surprising turn, it wasn't any of their impressive forward line who got the goal. The ball bounced around in the box before falling to defensive midfielder Idrissa Gueye, who blasted it into the top corner.

But that goal was against the run of play, as the rest of the game was all City – and they came close to scoring on a number of occasions.

Lionel often found himself a bystander, looking on as City launched attack after attack. When PSG did come forward, it usually went to Mbappé or Neymar. They weren't yet used to having Lionel with them.

But in the second half, he got his chance.

He came in from the right-hand side, moving into open space, as he'd done so often in his career. He spotted Mbappé's run and flicked the ball into him.

Mbappé was already in tune with Lionel and quickly moved the ball back into his path. Lionel met it straight away with a thunderous left-footed strike that flew into the top corner.

He'd doubled PSG's lead and got his first goal for the club.

It was the first time Lionel had ever scored for a club that wasn't Barcelona, and for a moment it felt very odd. But then the roar of the Paris crowd quickly settled him.

And as he celebrated with Mbappé and Neymar, he felt a level of optimism about the future that he hadn't had for years.

This was a team that he could win things with. He had an international trophy under his belt, he was playing well, he was scoring goals and he was feeling renewed. At 34 years of age, he was still as good as ever.

The criticisms and question marks that had been raised against him were beginning to fade now.

He was Lionel Messi, the best player of all time, and he was still going strong.

HOW MANY HAVE YOU READ?

 MESSI

 KANE

RONALDO

HAALAND

 SALAH

 PULISIC

 LEWANDOWSKI

 MAHREZ

 MBAPPÉ

 SON

 SAKA

 SANCHO

 FÉLIX

 GNABRY

 STERLING

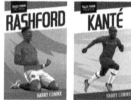 RASHFORD

 KANTÉ

 SILVA

 VAN DIJK

 SOUTHGATE

 GUARDIOLA

HARRY CONINX